CATCH A FIRE: Heal The Nation

IN PRAISE OF the ones that came before me…

"The advice I give to young people is fundamen-
tally to not let others put limits on who you
think you can be, to not put limits on them, and
to understand and to believe that all of us have
talents and have things to contribute. And my
father always taught us to aim for the stars so
that you can at least reach the tree tops, and
at any rate, you will get off the ground. And
his basic message is if you don't aim high, you
won't go far. But I say that knowing that many
young people have very difficult life circum-
stances and so on. But in the end, never let
others define what your life can be."

> – **Dr. Shirley Ann Jackson,**
> physicist and university
> president, quote from Black
> Scientist's Path To Success Was
> Often Lonely (2009)

"Your children are not your children. They are
the sons and daughters of Life's longing for itself. They come through you but not from you and
though they are with you yet they belong not to
you. You may give them your love but not your
thoughts, for they have their own thoughts. You
may house their bodies but not their souls, for
their souls dwell in the house of tomorrow,
which you cannot visit, not even in your dreams.

You may strive to be like them, but seek not to
make them like you. For life goes not backward
nor tarries with yesterday. You are the bows
from which your children as living arrows are
sent forth. The archer sees the mark upon the
path of the infinite, and He bends you with His
might that His arrows may go swift and far.
Let your bending in the archer's hand be for
gladness;
For even as He loves the arrow that flies, so He
loves also the bow that is stable."

> — **Khalil Gibran**, artist, poet,
> philosopher and author of The
> Prophet (1923)

"The term 'black' was given a rebirth by the
black youth revolt. As reborn, it does not refer
to the particular color of any particular person, but to the attitude of pride and devotion
to the race whose homeland from times immemorial
was called 'The Land of the Blacks.' Almost
overnight our youngsters made 'black' coequal
with 'white' in respectability, and challenged
the anti-black Negroes to decide on which side
they stood. This was no problem for many who are
light or even near-white in complexion, for they
themselves were among the first to proclaim with
pride, 'call me black!' Those who hate the term
but hold the majority of leadership positions
feel compelled to use it to protect their leadership roles."

— **Chancellor Williams,**
sociologist, historian and
author of Destruction of Black
Civilization: Great Issues of
Race From 4500 B.C. To 2000
A.D.

"Of the many inhuman outrages of this present
year, the only case where the proposed lynching
did not occur, was where the men armed themselves in Jacksonville, Fla and Paducah, Ky, and
prevented it. The only times an Afro-American
who was assaulted got away has been when he had
a gun and used it in self-defense. The lesson
this teaches and which every Afro-American
should ponder well, is that a Winchester rifle
should have a place of honor in every black
home, and it should be used for that protection
which the law refuses to give. When the white
man who is always the aggressor knows he runs as
great a risk of biting the dust every time his
Afro-American victim does, he will have greater
respect for Afro-American life. The more the
Afro-American yields and cringes and begs, the
more he has to do so, the more he is insulted,
outraged and lynched."

— **Ida B. Wells,** investigative
journalist, educator, civil
rights leader and author of
Southern Horrors: Lynch Law in
All Its Phases (1892)

"The laws of the dictatorial instruments of government have replaced the natural laws, i.e., positive law has replaced natural law. Consequently, ethical standards have become confused. The human being is essentially, physically and emotionally, the same everywhere. Because of this fact, natural laws are applicable to all. However, constitutions as conventional laws do not perceive human beings equally. This view has no justification, except for the fact that it reflects the will of the instrument of government, be it an individual, an assembly, a class or a party. That is why constitutions change when an alteration in the instruments of government takes place, indicating that a constitution is not natural law but reflects the drive of the instrument of government to serve its own purpose."

- **Muammar Gadaffi**, revolutionary, politician and author of The Green Book (1975)

CATCH A FIRE:

Heal the World

CJ CROCKETT

contents

acknowledgements

The seeds for this work were planted long ago by my parents falling in love; and even earlier than that with their parents. Ms. Dawkins, Ms. Pope, Mr. Givens, Mrs. Pyatt and Mr. Verrilli followed suit at 14th Avenue School and North Star Academy Charter School of Newark respectively. Research and learning through reading and conversing has always been a norm and it has rewarded me many things I am grateful for: the time well spent that is gone forever, the experiences money couldn't buy and memories I wouldn't sell for any amount. The dedication of those that inspired me compels my hand. From the moment I began writing I knew I would never stop.

PART 1
Ever Change

NURTURE HOPE

^

^

^

Walking through clouds
Higher than high
Not a gust of wind blowing
Not a bird in the sky
The further I go
The more I believe
There's something out there
My soul needs to see
My senses are on alert
Feeling for something extraordinary
You'd think I'd feel afraid
But there's nothing more contrary
A dove isn't hopeful
It simply flies as it should
I pray nothing tries to stop me
As if anything could
It feels like I've flown for hours
Carrying some sacred message within
Until I find what I seek
This journey will not end

ART: LIFE'S PORTRAIT

^

^

^

The watchful eye of the still

Handcrafted by the mind's image

Full of vibrant life and lush intimacy

Strokes and swipes, short and long

A manifestation of the mind's reach

Imagery from the inner core to be taken in
by any curious beholder

The passing traveler stops in his tracks to
appreciate the talent of one great thinker

Forgetting all strife and
sorrow for but
a moment its job is done

A million of these fractions of observances
is the method to ones crafty madness

Lashing clashes of blots, splashes and
swirls make up such a thing that
warms the heart and calms the brain
Curing the soul

Only a piece of artwork can achieve
Such a response from the unexpecting

A template of being, of mattering

The artist creates for all

No disclaimer for race or creed, just a
bold demand for a millisecond of attention
to ease, appease and evoke emotion

The traveler is now that much more in tune
with the world and the world with him

PATIENCE

^

^

^

I have questions and I have doubts
for what the outcome will bring
History has proven that all things
that start well don't end well
Ginger footsteps doesn't mean you won't
break the ice beneath your feet
But a mere crack doesn't mean
that all is over

Milling about aimlessly
in search of an answer
Predicting that it will come to no avail
For I know that I may not
recognize it when it does
My thoughts are stretched to my wits end
My ears seeking a whisper
My nostrils flaring wildly and
anxiously for a whiff
Dilated pupils
Hands outstretched
Lactic acid flowing

Nail biting moments creep by,
mocking the snail's trip
I'll just wait, sometimes you have to
As the clock strikes nine
I look myself over in the mirror
The fresh pump from the morning's workout
has my muscles on bulge
And there is only one thing on my mind
It is you

The rough and wet push and
pull of our natures,
Our give and take of the more
pleasurable things in life
Our bodies form a covenant
as I give all of me and
you take it in full
I grope you and you scratch me
I bite you and you scream out
allowing me to know the full extent
of your pleasure

We aren't fucking,
no it just appears that way
This is love
Me loving you and you loving me
No we are not in love,
But we are love

UNTITLED #3

^

^

^

If my children aren't proof that God exists
then this must all be a dream.
What is in a dream?

Over and under through true
waves of constant glee
as my first youth is born.
Bless.

Childbirth like these wondrous
things that cannot be grasped:
A cool flame, freedom,
steady weather in Boston,
the truth about God...

THE FAIR SHEEP

^

^

^

Rising and falling, I just watch as a heart
reaches for God.
Sleeping, my angel.
A dove of the purest kind.
White head crowning regally.
Noah's companion. Holy messenger.

If in God we trust we must
feed love and stay lust.
Our Lord, does see.

Righteousness, a gift of
the most black and beautiful hue.
One that absorbs light.

She is the embodiment of all your fears.

GODLY FAVOR

^

^

^

Unload an arsenal of the desperate
Let them drink a splash of the Queens nec-
tar Replace their tainted hearts with love
The darker side of the world comforts the
sleeping peoples while the sun appraises
the latter of the beautiful beings
Mahogany toned, melanin accented
The so called negro has divided itself
In each respect our glory of God determined
epidermis's shine
Even in its deepest hue
The black Acai berry is ever sweetened
by the heightened senses of the taster
Honey moves across the palate warmly
Calming the once stoaked fire
Milky cream butter of ever stretching love
intertwined with black beauty
and soft highlights quell
the most raucous of storms
All being a delicious jambalaya
that even the blandest tongued would envy.

BOOKWORM

^

^

^

A bookmark passes through the sheets
fingering along the sentences plane,
following the pages keep.

Understanding falls from the
book's spine inciting thought and
inquisitive curiosity.

The act of reading.

The sharing of life.

The mapping, framing, and stamping.

Reading is more than fundamental.

My eyes long for the experience.

The best things in life are free.

UNTITLED #1

^

^

^

In a lowland of bad thoughts and headaches
one can find refuge and solitude
in the small dark places of the brain,
beyond the crevices that hold
anger, despair, jealousy,
rage, envy and doubt
but amongst the flowers and lilies
of your inner child.

Chocolate, roses, rainbows and summer rains
A slow dance with me in your mind
your hand in mine
friends as friends should be
Honest and blunt,
accepting and forgiving.

STREAMS

^

^

^

Don't be afraid to lose yourself
in the music
Among the bullshit and
on top of the elements
put in place for your demise,
disguise yourself as
something you are not.

Stand a huge monument of courage, power
and fury on the outside,
while on the inside come lay with me.

Allow your body to float alongside mine
weightless and free of worry
down these streams.

UNTITLED #2

^

^

^

Cover the world in a lover's warmth and allow us all a pass.

Dodging worrisome thoughts of missed oppor-
tunities and
the reality of time wasted.

Soak in a man like me and reap the rewards
of patience and understanding.

Allow your past to find the back seat and
strap it in for the journey because the re-
volving door finally brought you something
you could chew.

Test the waters.

No, tread them and find a shark.

Rains reign raising seas,
convincing the sun to hide.

The advice of fools.

Manipulation stacked against fast times.

My steps reflect the dream's end.

Steady, sure and forward as the seasons.

At the brink of the changing of tides when
the mountains have moved and the sun's
glare allows a clear view.

We can clearly see the important message
that was lost in the midst of the battle.

Pressurize the care and love that the able
mind and beating heart is capable of to the
highest measure and find some use for it.

There are a plethora of choices.

Oh, how beautiful the music is.

FOOD FOR THOUGHT

^

^

^

Alone and afraid but in heaven here with
sharks that circle around

Wanting what I want, more
Sure I can find something
It always provides

The sun above, whew
Cooking and unyielding and
It continues on

I dangle my feet for short periods of time
I never gamble

The sound of the sea unwinds me and
loves me back
Life teems beneath me

Compass-less, I'm fine
Never alone here
Looking for myself

WILL

^

^

^

In search of new lands I build a new house
upon a foundation of will.

This house is not a home but a temporary
cerebral shelter and a permanent sanctuary
where I could possibly thrive.

The walls are stuccoed to hold in the
heat from my body's energy so that it en-
compasses the space around
my mind when it's released.

Colloquially discussing
my plans with nature,
I get feedback from the bowing of the
tree's limbs and the smell and
sound of the rising sun.

I look out farther beyond what I can perceive and see truer.
The haze is just fear.

Now settling into the outer parts of what
is me I force myself to remember and
to forget the best of the worst days.

I reach out at the densely barked trees.
I breathe in the crisp air.
I look down at my reflection
in the river and
remember what I am here for.

Courage reaches through the blackest darkness and snatches at your coattails.

No one is chasing you.
You're just headed in the wrong direction.

HOME

^

^

^

I walked out of the door and far from the
house on this night,
a cool breeze touched my skin

Not a car on the road or a person in sight
I find humor in this and grin

If not for the low hanging moon and
Strangely reaching branches
I would feel alone and
usually this eerie feeling
would force me back home

Yet I walk on and on
Taking in the evening air
Not veering from my course
I don't even know to where

Over the crack that broke mama's back
Pass the boot imprinted on the cement
Between the fiend's lean and the sidewalk
and beyond the apartment where
we couldn't afford rent

I hear voices and I see
faces as if the street is alive
I even watch a ball game between
some friends that died

This street is a book of
lost children who still thrive
This is our reality here
From where do you derive?

MORE THAN JAZZ

^

^

^

Poems just before dawn
Cannonball Adderley & Bill Evans
play for Nancy
I think of someone else

The piano and horn is still justified
Her laughing face always means so much more
Hell, we're still dancing

I never get the feeling that I'm falling
Chilean reds swirling in our glasses
I'm drowned in everything that she is

In her absence, Coltrane fills the void
Naima's piano and horn jerks at me
It's the only time I cry

DEVIL'S SNARE

^

^

^

He whispered,
"Go on. Home is where the heart is.
You never have to come back here again."
Then, he asked me to trust him
to take care of my people.
The words sweetened the longer it spoke.
I warned myself about choices and
the weight they bore and
I pondered on his intention.
Yet, I still made the wrong
decision and now we're here.
Fighting daily to stay woke.

BLESSINGS

^

^

^

You don't have to worry about the storm
rolling in behind the dark clouds.

Rainfall brings sunshine,
a natural rejuvenation of life.

I find myself relaxed in my arm chair
when the elephant drops off a daytime rain
spell in the spring and it eases by.

In bed, in a deep state of hibernation when
the night brings continuous thunderstorms
in the summer.

Lightning flashes confirm that the
lights upstairs are on so sleep child
for no harm shall fall upon you tonight.

God is sprinkling blessings.

FACING GOD

^

^

^

Thrice I saw God
A gathering of lovers
There was a bright light
Two reaching hands
Creations created
There was no booming voice but people spoke
There were no cheers but we were all happy
Although we all cried
Three times I saw God
When my children were born

SUICIDE: SELF-MUTILATION

^

^

^

a shade everlasting
a dim light teases my irises
a comfort from the harshest
of the sun's rays
I so fear the missing of a new sunrise

i read somewhere
"I die at night and awake
a new man at first light"
but i fear, I fear the biting off of
more than I can chew
"What of it?" I yell.
"Fuck it?"

overstand or fall short living
but not feeling alive.
is it a good way to die?

TROUBLED MAN

^

^

^

Too little too late, too much too soon so
it gave me migraines and head colds.

Having no faith in you with a
mind full of cloudy thoughts,
a heart filled with love and
a mouthful of accusations.

Your reasoning liquefied your excuses
mounting my endearment of
you with frustration.

"But why," was my most voiced plea.

Every time I hear a love ballad I switch it
to something harder.

I can't slow-groove to something I can't
feel.

Won't feel.

Seal black is the tortilla
that wraps my heart.

Edible at first glance but it'll choke you.

Two strong hands around the throat.

A threat that ceases to quit.

Scars boil over a stoked fire
causing them to swell.

A marred appearance to anyone paying attention So look deeper and remove the
fitted sheet that covers my fears.

I'm always dodging bullets and waiting for
a reason to make my exit
Each time through the front door.

So, let the music play.

Half the time I'm not listening.

PART 2
What Is Real

DYING TO LIVE

^

^

^

I was born to die
Indefinitely someday
I'm dying to live
Getting closer each day
Detached from the falsehoods
I've righted my wrongs
Fallen in love twice
The sweet truth in a song
Falling deep into trances
Daydreams of what death could bring
A silhouette of black fears
I've worried about lesser things
Fit to live but living to die
Wondering how one could be so torn
Deaf with ears, blind with eyes
Trying to figure out why I was born

UNTITLED #4

^
^
^

Slowly spooning my oatmeal
thinking how my bland
breakfast could use some more sugar.

My kitchen table is a crowded
plateau of wayward thoughts and
memories crashing into each other.

Raw sweetened reminiscences push a flowing
tingle from the back of my neck down
through my body, pumping blood
filled with hot lust and longing.

I think I put too much water in this shit!

Werewolf sightings of this
most potent poison,
I long for it to course through my veins.
Inject me with a hit of corrosive eye con-
tact; sweet sounding body language.

I should've added more milk.

Unzip all tainted memories to once again
be engulfed in that thing that
felt so good at one time before.
Before the oceans waves pulled you ever
further from the island
on which we dwelled.
Far away from the have-nots and the hungry.

I've got to reheat this crap.

Pink plush pillows. Zebra print love.
Candy tainted truths and bold expressions
of cliche sentences that dull the senses.
Water trickles through the smallest of
holes, as does the heart.

Never mind. I lost my appetite.

OVERCOME

^

^

^

Chastised by blackness and
buried deep in its wake
The walls have closed in and the
weight from my own head sways me
Dizziness warps my wits and
all becomes black
Total and utter darkness
A peep! I would hear a mere flutter and
my ears would arrest but there is nothing
Doesn't anything dare fight back?
Fangless and without claw, I stand
hunch-backed since the ceiling is low
I feel something warm inside
Giving me strength and running
hot lines of courage to my joints
My vision screams at my sanity,
fighting the pits of malevolence
I begin to punch, kick, thrash and
tear my way out of that existence
I can no longer fit in
There is no fierce menacing roar
louder than my own
as I break from my shell

CREATION

^
^
^

Twice I saw God
A gathering of lovers
There was a bright light
Two reaching hands
Creations created
There was no booming voice but people spoke
Their were no cheers but we were all happy
although we all cried
Twice I saw God
when my children were born

POINT, BLANK...

^

^

^

Hating my body
because of what it must do.
Being a woman.

I hear her talk and
I can't really understand
But I do listen

The endless cycle
Just as crucial as it is
Painful and tasteless.

WORLD OF STRIFE

^

^

^

My tattoos don't cover my battle scars but
it's all in the same plane as
black boxes and strangers.
It's hard to comprehend,
no matter how sane the claim.
We're not close but
we're still neighbors.
Take what you want,
just give me what I need.
War torn countries without
any tears left to grieve.
Still some people need access,
a view from the inside so they
can smell their own shit and
let the fantasies die.
There's not a drink or a drug that
can out sound the babies' cry.
What's normal changes based on
your pay and stifled pride.

POWER

^

^

^

5 miles from empty
Under the influence of losing momentum
Teetering on the edge of gaining
understanding and letting go of it all
Mobilized fear of never gracing
the glory of something that no longer ex-
ists though I can still…
Feel its warmth,
Smell its breath,
Hear its voice

My world is foot stepping on the ceiling
The surface level of my sanity
in its pocket
I am determined to be free
from my mind's prison
I am tied without knot,
chained without lock
It's up to me
to make the hurt stop

FAITHFUL

^

^

^

All the world's a stage!

Show your face and scream your name,

Without your shoes on.

STRANGER FRUITS

^

^

^

All Hallows Eve ghouls walk
in hand with Christmas Saints?
It must be the Fourth!

Black magic bordered faith.
Symbols, signs and tied fortunes.
Dare not to escape.

Seed born from the plague yet
choice is born to us all
Be better than them,
arranged in display
Broken, twisted, and beautiful

Where is your God now?

CHECKERED FLAGS

^

^

^

Attitude to match a bull's tenacity and
enough pressure to return
a diamond to coal,
I blaze roads uncharted.

Outer space is the limit and
even there my dreams will stay afloat.
No longer committing to conformity,
up is where I aim my drive.

Off course but steadily on track.
Treaded tires to match any terrain. Ensur-
ing my grip is strong and
that I am well equipped with what's
necessary to gain ground.

The sun is at apex and
feeding me in my bout.
Everything that could be,
will be and all will
be made right.

SOULMATES

^

^

^

In pitch darkness she is calling out
Branches snap and twigs snap under
my feet as I follow her
voice in pitch blackness
Alone
All alone and she's calling out
Her drumming heartbeat leads me to her
in pitch blackness
Wide tree boughs hang low
to decapitate me, alive and engulfing
The world around me squeezes down
It's pulls at me
Strips me of my clothes
Money bears no purpose here, only will
The will to go on
in pitch blackness
Her voice grows stronger
We grow closer
I become something different knowing this
I am not afraid because she is not afraid
She is calling out and she knows
I am coming for her

UNTITLED #6

^
^
^

When you stop living a lie,
that's freedom

You need not to try to find
the soul in your reflection

It's just a casted image

Less than alive and deprived

Don't let go of what makes you real.

ROMEO

^

^

^

I was wondering...
Could I part the sea for you or
am I too forward?
Heartening.
Higher than a bird,
I nosedive into their hate
Catch me with your love.

Double trouble and terrors in kind.
Vile and wretched lot.
Sadistically sane.
She smells like something I've seen before.
She hears my thoughts.
Meeting all criteria, a smoking Dillinger
Hot! Hotter than oven baked cakes
Cover this love thang
She drives so sweetly
Sings with no voice
Bridging the stage, the curtains are drawn
Ice me up sugar baby

AS IS

^

^

^

A satirical play for educational purposes
Our game was won and loss
A search in time for
something to take me back
Pure notions of interest spread over numer-
ous introductions,
where I knew my taste had
finally been engaged

Seeing things as one,
smiling together, as two…
pillow top loving and
climaxing in threes
What was it all for?

Four arguments every three days
to find balance for two
All because fate brought you someone
Yet memories don't lie and all of my senses
think fondly of you

My taste remains the same
I hear your heart song
lingering in my ear drum
I can still see your shadow on the ground,
overlapping mine,
when I walk down the neighborhood pass our
favorite places

Feeling the warmth and smoothness
of your palm upon my forearm
I smell your perfume
fused in with your scent
The taste of God's gift to a mere man

Will God hear these words?
Will he relay them?

The world still spins bringing
days and people anew
As long as the sky stays blue
I'll still be in love with you

PEPPERED

^

^

^

Lights please, since
this conversation is over
I riffed my retort with muscles bulging
in my neck and veins tight
Storming from the room feeling vindicated
after another shouting match
Love, common sense,
dishonesty and vigilance
Hotter than July at the fact
that you force me to reveal my inner emotions and unveil
a less gentlemanly exterior
I'm even madder at the reality that
after days pass…text messages,
early morning and late night phone calls
lead me back to your bed
And that's the extent of my
happiness with you, the sex
I'm still not happy
I'm still not satisfied with you
I'm still not satisfied without you
What the fuck is this?

TOGETHER

^

^

^

There is only one thing on my mind and
it is you
The rough and wet push and
pull of our natures
Our give and take of the more
pleasurable things in life
Our bodies form a covenant

As I give all of me, you take it in full
I grope, you scratch,
I bite and you scream out
You care for me to know the
full extent of your pleasure
We aren't fucking, no
it just appears that way
This is love
We are in love with ourselves and
that is okay

We are love and we will last

INFLICTION

^

^

^

These days people are as faithful as their options. It's what I've been shown, nothing more. A person's loyalty to a friend can only be as mature as the loyalty to themselves. A person's fidelity to you is unyielding when they feel they have no on else. That is up until, of course, someone else comes along. Then the tales become taller and the agitation grows greater. You see the falsehood of their new facades and you still allow yourself to be stretched and compromised. What is the purpose? It's one in the same with self-mutilation.

I Am A Man

^

^

^

Quiet whispers over honey graham kisses
Sweet tones of love's message flowing
Into my ear drums from your lips
Your soft hands upon my head
As you finger my earlobe telling me
of things you've dreamt of
I am nothing like what your
parents wanted and quite the opposite of
your prince charming
Still the record replays itself
without break and the ice in
our teas have melted
Hot summer air cools
the sweat on our bodies
Fresh linen sheets smell of
bright days and city bound evenings
I kiss her lips for
words can't describe the
Regal comfortable state I lounge in
I am atop Mount Everest
With this queen in my luxury
I kiss her feet in humility
I kiss her hands in thanks

MOMENTS IN LOVE

^

^

^

Moments in love captured in the
faintest of memories,
Now lost amid the flaps of a dove's wings
Graceful but quick and flighty.
In an instance compassion explores my inner
body looking for a place to land.
With help from my deep
inhaled breaths I can blow away the footsteps in the sand.
The time turns slowly so the
moments feel like an eternity.

I hear my heart beat in my eardrum
As it reverberates through my love bones.
It speaks volumes to my hidden despair,
though I don't recognize it as such
So I fold it upon itself, to be tucked back
into the place where
I know it can't hurt me.

These moments in love are short and much
too few and far in between.

NIGHT NURSE

^

^

^

Hunger pangs my insides causing a calamity

I cease to think clearly in an effort
to stop the cravings

My voracious appetite grows ever stronger
as I search high and
low for this strange fruit

Sweet Berry centered and peachy pink
I can taste it, I can smell it

Wrapped up in memories of pleasantries,
my loins constrict as if
inflicted with venom

Hot acid-like seeping ever slowly
like the tortoise's crawl

That medicinal get down to which
I am addicted
It is time for our dosage

The sway of lucid clarity
In and out of the state between soul fill-
ing anguish and the
rise of the next sun

Chastised by threats of bliss,
I am flogged with past experiences of this
nurse's healing powers

Syringes filled to the tip
ready to be expended
Into my love stream

My night nurse is always good to me

My night nurse

My night nurse

My night nurse

PART 3
Finding Our Way

SWEET CHILD

^

^

^

Feel free to walk up on me Sweet Child.
Ask me why I'm staring at you so.
Hell, simply ask me for directions and
I'll be a happy man.
Maybe I should ditch my watch and
ask you for the hour.
Ask you for the time when I can simply
check my cellular device.
Someone as grand as you
I must exchange words with.
The light toned locks of love that grace
your shoulders talk to me;
extensions of you.
That sway of yours grasped my attention
first then your smooth skin accented.
Those lips, those soft lips,
easy-going sea colored vivacious eyes,
those eyes…tastefully you attract me.
Never mind the sexual thoughts.
Forget the curve of your behind,
the dip in the small of your back and
the roundness of your breasts.

I just want to be close enough
to take in your scent.
Right there long enough to
hear your voice sing into my ears.
Just to meet your acquaintance and speak to
you thoroughly and truthfully.
To see where you are from.
To see what you are about.
Cause right now, as the cocks crow and the
dogs bark, you're the cat's meow.
Purr baby, purr.
That glow you have could only mean that you
are a special child of God.
And those freckles...star flakes.
You intrigue me even more now.
When you look at me it's rhythmic.
A sing-song beautiful kind of music.
Talk to me, sweet child.
At least whisper in my direction.

LIVING WITH WOMEN

^

^

^

Glutton for love
Treat me as your heart
Batter me with lures of hope
Give me a beating.

Sick
That's the way love goes but
I want it no longer
Allow me to go.

To love or not to
I'd rather prepare for spring
Love is a ground hog
Skip summer and remember to
Put that fucking toilet seat down.

BELIEVE

^

^

^

Black magic bordered,
Faith. Symbols, signs, tied fortunes.
Dare not to escape

The manifestation of goals is
an action of pros
free from the fear of woes,
overcoming the most
wicked of foes.

If in God we trust
We must feed love and stay lust
Our lord, Savior.
God's Gift
Over and under
Through true waves of constant glee
As my first child is born.

HEAVEN'S SAKE

^

^

^

Bones built to carry
Nature's bountiful life-fruit
Out of touch with self

Here in front of me
Glowing in its purest form, unsullied
A dying angel

THE STUDENT

^

^

^

I will teach you the ways
of women and the ways of men

I will teach you how to stay afloat
when you're afraid to swim

I will teach you how to fight
when you're tired and spent

I'll teach you how to let
the bullshit stay wherever it went

I will teach you what it means
to stand on your own

I will teach you why
you should never feel down and alone

I will teach you what
my parents could not teach me

I will teach you to
feel for the things you cannot see

I will teach you how to predict
the weather by the scent in the air

I will teach you the reason why
you should always care

I will teach you with soft words
I will teach you without rod

I will teach you what it means
to be alive and seek God

THAT OUTER SPACE

^

^

^

Open on all accords, just play
Tattooed mission to gather what
I'm missing and just slay

Delectable delights on my tongue
Sweet letters that make words dance and run

Touch with my eyes since my hands are tied
Seeking those feelings heavily underlined

A flow that move oceans, unsupervised
Anything that interrupts this motion I
strongly deny

On top of the world and
ready to lay under it
Added lightening that can be frightened,
lost in its wonderment

The strongest foundation bending,
swaying at me
As if one could lay hands on the surface
and still the sea

Blend the divine with the sublime and
be rewarded
Spend this life source up
for another and afford it

Saddle up a spaceship to prove
once and for all
For this love,
to the deepest depths I'll fall

FIRSTS

^

^

^

Hell, this thing will never go away,
I'm okay with that
When the day in the future comes when
we have no words to say,
I'm gonna wanna go back

With all the barking at and fighting with
Felled tears from trying it
Your slide shit and my lying trips
had us both on some crying shit

Feeling justified like
"Oh, you wanna be a playa, have that!"
Too far gone is a woman scorned
I guess our dope shot
from cupid was a bad batch

Even still the love was real
I got burned by a lesson learned and
I still don't know how I feel

So I charge it to the game
I'm satisfied knowing that
you will never forget my name

Forever you will love my voice
You really don't have a choice

Like when I hear a song and
can smell your scent
Reminding me of the moments
that were well spent

These new days we do what gets us through
You were once a rock for me
I softened those hard places for you

How can I not still be weak for the one
that helped me surf the sky?
You were the one who
sung my first child's lullaby

Memories will live on,
hoping the bad one choose not to stay
Hell, this thing will one day fade away

LIVE AND LET LIVE

^

^

^

Dress me down in the finest linens so
I can fight the dirtiest war.

Swear in a slew of the newest born so
that my army is just.

Sling a bouquet of roses across my back
so that our mothers are pleased.

Rotate the wheels on all the wagons,
paint them green and
douse them in spirits.

Cringe at the bay of our
battle ready horns,
the deep pounds of our drums.

Let fruit fly from our mouths
as we sing up high into the skies
a song of victory before
the first blade even pierces the air.

See what we cannot for what we can
is already written.

Last of all, bless us.
Bless us with the courage to push on
after all we know and even love is gone.

Great things smell like pie,
the window seal's company.

Let the horse's eat.

REAP

^

^

^

Permanently inked, the marks of a warrior
Damn, this thing itches.
Dogs, willing and able
to please without argument
What more to ask for?

The void, nevertheless cold
The hand strikes twelve, just silence
Nothingness is here.

Cage the Elephant
It does not fear mice or man.
Why the hell should it?

Something Inside burns
Read not what it says but
understand the message.
Let us all a stare.

Get the big picture and
be better off without
I live heartless and survive on
You only live once, right?

THE PIPER

^
^
^

My scars remind me that the past is real
They still bleed out
Despite all the time they've had to heal
I'll soon recover, there is no doubt

Irreparable damage leaks weakening venom
Gashes and slits burn where
I put salt in them

Medicate, stitch, bandage and wrap
Harm's way is always mine as well
Because of the fear I lack

My epidermis is pissed off
My immune system screams
My spine won't let me stand straight
My stomach blasphemes all kinds of things

The medicine wears too fast
The stitches unravel
The bandage slides and the wrap tears
with every step I travel

Ramming my fingers into the hurt
I'm down to my wrist
Through unbearable pain
I dig deeper into it

Clenching my teeth and
Squeezing my eyes shut,
I'm temporarily blinded
When you do wrong, you pay the piper
I'm daily reminded

POSITIVELY

^

^

^

Do we become Gods as we grow or
is it always in our hearts
And of course your at fault for not
giving a shit from the start
Tired of junkies, colored flags,
the word fag and those who only
pretend to be smart

A new heavy focus on this world disease and
why the hoods aren't growing
Why is everybody dying and
everybody knowing?

Why is it always heat on my block,
even when it's snowing?
Why do we need gangs when a
family's blood line is still flowing?

Fucking rapists chased and
maimed Us
They're the reason why
we know what hatred is

Over coerced, heart broken and cursed
It's exactly why we treat
our own selves the worst

Why boys take to the streets and
girls take to the sheets
Cause the family is not a home and
the media is the beast

Conditioned like my
little sisters black mane
I'm asking that we put the gats down and
grasp hands, especially non-friends
Because to win we must love our enemy and
To overcome to bullshit we need good energy

FATHOM

^
^
^

Sickened and suffering and
now I got a remedy
Dud out my Mary Jane, put down the Hennessy
Bad Guy Syndrome, those
broken hearts remember me
Pandora's box spilled over and
it's way too slippery
Now I want a real queen and
everything is peasantry
Got a good grip on this fat ass but
can't grasp no quality
They want money, they want drugs
Red button, don't bother me
My old girls are happy
Praying the worlds going to swallow me
Please say y'all kidding me,
Loving when I'm in misery?
My vision is clear and my mind is sane
I solved my own trickery
Sober soul and a pot of gold
I swear my baby momma's it for me but she
say its too late
I shit on her so she split on me

But come on, that ain't it for me
I'm getting to where I'm meant to be
Shackled down with no chains
I'll bring the whole damn ship with me

So I'm tying up my black boots and
Zipping up my black jacket
Just finished riding my black chick
Restocking all my black ratchets
I'm blackin out
Since 'blackin' is in
Finding cowards and attacking them
Damn the streets, drugs and tests
Damn police that cause more stress
Damn the block for being there
The system know and they don't care
Im taking this in my own hands
Bite the bullet to feed my fam
Imma burn it all down
More than enough gas cans
This ain't even my fucking land
Honest Mom, have you heard from God?
To free my people l'll give my heart

HIS STORY

^

^

^

The burning morning sky is under new rule
Empty fabric lay cast aside
Lifeless atop a man's, shoulders
Burdened and forsaken
All of the daughters have been lost
The sons are here but they are no more
The clouds cry to no avail
Even the sun burns blue
The mask is the true image

The ritual of birth, growth, and ascension
dissipates as it is cut down,
stripped, boiled and
eaten but not ingested
The old woman screamed for the gods
The old man called for the spear
The wife, for her husband
The child, for his mother
The earth, for time

Here in black,
I try daily to forget about slavery
to no avail

Bitterness growing knowing that
the entire lives of most was a literal hell
My race of people were hung, raped and bat-
tered just 70 years ago
That's one lifetime

What should be remembered?
What should be taught?
What should be forgotten? If anything.
Images flash in my mind
I can't really even begin to fathom the up-
rooting of a culture
How is that possible?
How was it that easy?
Maybe these native peoples
were benevolent by nature
Undoubtedly guilty of being
trusting and loving
America is the home of
the stolen and the deceived and
most are abused and dejected
How is our memory so short?

Allow us to breathe life
back into a great people
The revelation will be who we are to become
The peoples kept at the bottom
with nothing left to lose
can only gain

BATTLE HILL

^
^
^

Stimulated by what's inside
fighting to get out
If it wins, I win
The only obstacle in my way
is the mind's doubt
With that I grin
Me vs me? How could I lose?
I'm fully equipped with
the tools I need to use
Taking orders from a high society
we are not apart of
Never mind having guards up
we're all wearing blinders
The revolution just might be televised
God bless what Gil said
I realized I should've listened to every-
thing I was told by the old heads
You see because plenty has happened
But not much has changed
The corners on my son's way to school
still look the same
The number streets are still hot
Mamas are still losing babies

A kid got killed by his cousins last night
Now their uncle is talking crazy
Barack Obama is not our savior
though he's a good man
A boss does what he wants,
not what he can
The revolution will be televised
Because everyone will have a part in it
I have a vivid picture of the venture
in my head and I'm loving it
I was raised to never let up on what
I believe in but they forgot to tell me
all the bullshit I'd be in
They told me the caresser
could also be doing the oppressing
I didn't know I'd have to suffer
this much for a blessing
As the slope evens out
the road gets more slippery
We need action to make traction and
ensure serendipity

IN PEACE

^
^
^

From the crickets to the rainfall the
night is saying something to me

Waves of anger deep inside,
it's my ancestors walking through me

I sit with my eyes closed like my
great grandmother is talking to me

She said,
"All they have for you is a
speedy and public trial by jury."

Rest assured that I was listening,
squinting my eyes like she was televised

Giving me game how she lived
in a time I wouldn't have survived

Turn the other cheek?

I swear you wouldn't catch me alive

Kissing hands and scrubbing boots
of a wicked foreign invader
that I despise

Will this rain ease the pain?

Could the sound of these
crickets do the same?

The stars in the sky are glistening,
I wonder if God is listening

To these prayers I'm whispering to
my brother I'm missing

ADULTERY

^

^

^

Taking them in twos
Or threes if by club; no sweat
No care for substance
Deep.
My hands on her ass
I pull her to me roughly
The plunge stays her voice
Yes!
Hottest sex since slaves
You welcome these whips and cuffs
Hell, you'll plead for more.

SHIPWRECKED

^

^

^

In this moment of clarity
it all makes sense
She's under me moaning,
telephoning the good Lord
From this lust-filled bed,
hot pleasure digging through her sanity

Allowing her guards a rest,
I dig deep to find the place where her
ocean's waves smash against
the rock hard coast
I surf. Land Ho!
Gripping the sides so I can stay aboard

As I crest and fall with
the rhythm she's set
She's giving back, so I give front
Angling my endeavors to bring down torren-
tial rain
Baby, this ain't sex,
we're on a voyage
Across the uncharted sea of fucking and
it ain't no anchors

I'm churning up the jeweled cavern bottom
Coins turn over and
down ruby crusted necklaces
Rings endowed with great diamonds roll down
mounds of royalties
The warmth outside gives light to the fire
dwelling inside
Ever growing as it's being stoked
Cheeky plush dollars getting heavy change

In this moment of clarity
it all makes sense
She's under me moaning,
telephoning the good Lord
From this lust-filled bed,
hot pleasure digging through her sanity

STREAK OF LIGHT

^

^

^

I feel so much like everyone and
so different at the same time.
Overloaded with so many internal thoughts
I need a spare mind.

Tired and overworked,
sometimes I need a break from mine.
My brain is moving at a sprinter's pace
as I chase down time.

Learning from others' mistakes
is a gift in itself
Choosing action over words in
my goal to claim riches and wealth.

Hot stoves cooked up
what starved the family I love
So hard drugs was easily
something I never dug.

Stories of people who were under under and
what saved their life.
After lonely holidays and
punishing stone cold nights.

Make it like I lived through it with them,
never to make the same choices twice
Watched so many people feast at
the table and now I got a slice.

The world is changing,
Superman in the booth fast.
Watching before I switch lanes and
hoping I don't finish last.

Pushing to work ever harder
to seize the moment for progress but getting out of my own way
has been the hardest process.

Predicting my gain and
counting all my losses,
it seems like I can't print enough resumes
to catch the attention of these bosses.

Sometimes I sit back and
watch the world spin,
after dumping my job applications
in the trash bin.

Shit I can barely breathe
without someone aiming
to bring me to my knees
and it hurts trying to
fight back the anger,
trying to stifle a sneeze.

But if I don't,
verdict is I can't control my emotions,
mixed up masked feelings
as unpredictable as the ocean.

Minus the sea of life,
I'd prefer the clouds to speak tonight and
the morning brings what
the night clings onto,
a streak of light.

EFFORT

^

^

^

If she could read my mind her panties would
dissolve in her own wetness.
The images of my endeavors would bring a
man to nocturnal emission,
as he stands awake.
Those casaba melons for breasts collab with
her full lips in such a manner that it's
only right that I fix a taste for pineapple
so that my flow tastes good.
Innovative ways to make my member arise,
to keep him at attention.
I'd never think that pink over and in between brown would be so enticing.
So deliciously paired together, one in
the midst of two. Snugly.
My mouth waters with you.
Must I peak and come down?
Can we not elevate and levitate amidst the
full swing of the beautiful
clothless dance when my libido
forces out your crescendo?
Endure my weight under duress
and the relief will send bountiful

spurts of unfathomed satisfaction from
the ends of your strands of hair
to the bottom of your feet,
up through your cortex and
out into the cosmos.
I don't think that hot lava
has ever been fondled like this.
Let me do the things that only
I know how to do
These things that take you to
places unheard of
The places that women dream about,
the place you long to be
I can take you there but will you follow
Follow me to stroke, pull, lick,
fuck, suck and dig
Let me explore and find these places
in between and underneath your cloak of
attitude and pride, relieving strife
I can soothe your pain and
cause more with the pleasure I bring
Wrap those legs around me and let me feed
Can you handle it? Are you game?
Have no fear in what brings the good
Take me as I am and inhale deeply,
for here I stand naked, exposing my nature
My manhood stiffening as I speak to you
Ready, willing and able to do
all the good things you request of me

QUEENLY CHARACTER

^

^

^

She allowed me five seconds between her
knees to stay her mind and
change the way she breathed
Never ceasing to rub on her
as she touched on me
Both our minds have been hijacked since I
saw her fly and she felt my G
Only patient knees now
keep her legs at ease
Anxiously, she's forced to wait for me

It was intermittent but
I commenced to hitting without delay
To my surprise, she let me joy ride
knowing I don't play
Took the main road and the backstreet
Not a sign in sight saying 'wrong way'
Knocking deep waves through it
It sounded so close to music
you could confuse it

My back stroke enough
to make an Olympian choke

Slow poked and gently
prodded with pride by my rod
She screamed for God
exclaiming she never felt so alive
Between short gasps of air
I'm exhaling longevity
This mindless synced overflow
is sexual telepathy
Her eyes are all I see
Girl, got good sense…
smelling, touching and tasting me.
She's so bright and this room is dark
Explosive nature so it's no rush,
I prolong the spark
Over and under, inside and out,
chastising her middle
Wear it out.
Let me taste your tongue
since I've lost touch
I'm patiently impatient so
she don't tease me much
Her dirtiest little secrets,
she whispers to the King
Only thing I know is,
it's good to know the Queen

FIN

Made in the USA
Middletown, DE
29 September 2021